Weird and Wonderful

Dartmoor

Sally and Chips Barber

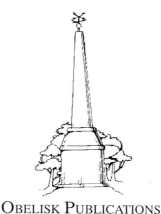

OBELISK PUBLICATIONS

ALSO BY SALLY & CHIPS BARBER
Dark & Dastardly Dartmoor
Ten Family Walks on Dartmoor
The Ghosts of Exeter

Other Dartmoor Titles
The Great Little Dartmoor Book, *Chips Barber*
Diary of a Dartmoor Walker, *Chips Barber*
Dartmoor in Colour, *Chips Barber*
Under Sail Through South Devon & Dartmoor, *R. B. Cattell*
The Great Walks of Dartmoor, *Terry Bound*
The A to Z of Dartmoor Tors, *Terry Bound*

OTHER OBELISK PUBLICATIONS INCLUDE:
Tales of the Teign, *Chips Barber & Judy Chard*
The Ghosts of Berry Pomeroy Castle, *Deryck Seymour*
The Ghosts of Torbay, *Deryck Seymour*
The Ghosts of Brixham, *Graham Wyley*
Haunted Happenings in Devon, *Judy Chard*
Tales of the Unexplained in Devon, *Judy Chard*
Exeter in Colour, *Chips Barber*
Torbay in Colour, *Chips Barber*
Plymouth in Colour, *Chips Barber*
The Great Little Plymouth Book, *Chips Barber*
The Great Little Exeter Book, *Chips Barber*
The Great Little Totnes Book, *Chips Barber & Bill Bennett*
Around & About the Haldon Hills, *Chips Barber*
The Lost City of Exeter, *Chips Barber*
Diary of a Devonshire Walker, *Chips Barber*
Burgh Island & Bigbury Bay, *Chips Barber & Judy Chard*
Made in Devon, *Chips Barber & David FitzGerald*

Plate Acknowledgements

Barry Hall, Page 7 (lower)
All drawings, and cover, by Jane Reynolds
All photographs taken by Chips Barber or from his collection of old photographs

For further details of any of our titles, please contact us at the address below or
telephone Exeter (0392) 68556

First published in 1991 by
Obelisk Publications, 2 Church Hill, Pinhoe, Exeter, Devon
Designed by Chips and Sally Barber
Edited and Typeset by Sally Barber
Printed in Great Britain by Penwell Ltd, Kelly Bray, Callington, Cornwall

Weird and Wonderful Dartmoor

Dartmoor's Dancing and Dining Trees

Imagine a great and ancient elm tree minding its own business, apart from little boys and girls occasionally clambering up it, and some bright spark thinks to himself, 'What a wonderful specimen – we could hold dances in that tree.' And so a platform is placed in the tree with room for a small band of musicians and space for locals to dance and make merry.

Unlikely? Well, this is precisely what happened at Moretonhampstead and the tree's fame spread far and wide. Devonshire vicar's son, Richard Doddridge Blackmore, who wrote *Lorna Doone,* included it in his *Christowell,* citing some of the advantages of holding a dance up a tree: 'Frisking among the verdure without the dread of dewy feet or toes stuck in a mole-hole'. Well put sir! Alas this great tree, also referred to as 'The Punchbowl Tree', was badly damaged in one snow storm then finished off by another storm in 1903.

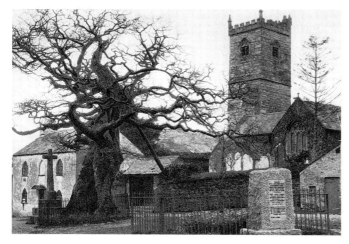

At the village of Meavy, on the south western side of Dartmoor, is a splendid oak which gives its name to the Royal Oak pub beside it. This venerable oak is said to be older than the nearby church. The story goes that the ravages of time have hollowed this tree, which is twenty six feet in circumference, and that on one occasion nine people dined within it.

The School Drum

Early this century, Meavy's village school was threatened with closure, a deed which would have forced its children to walk to Walkhampton. However the villagers, led by the vicar, cleared a parcel of land, given by the Lord of the Manor, and built a new school, having redirected funds intended for the building of a hall. Each day, instead of calling the children into class by the traditional bell, a copy of Drake's Drum was beaten, an act that was deemed most significant as Drake had lived only a few miles away at Buckland Abbey – where Drake's Drum is still kept.

The Great Edwardian Fountain at Moretonhampstead

What is the connection between Yellowstone National Park and Moretonhampstead in the early years of the twentieth century? The answer is a spectacular aquatic display. The difference though was Moretonhampstead's geyser-like performance was man-made, purely by accident, irregular and a health risk!

The Victorians made great progress in improving water supply and sanitation so, although Moreton was a little late in getting there, the relevant authorities did eventually do something. Two nine-inch pipes were laid down in each of two smaller tributary valleys of the River Wrey. In between, and on the ridge, was the town of Moreton. A simple piece of applied maths should have suggested that when the flow from these two nine-inch pipes joined, a larger pipe would be needed to accommodate the increased through put. Alas this was not done, the problem being exacerbated whenever a storm broke, as torrents of water flushed through the system. Consequently the storm water was sufficient to burst the pipes at their junction. As this happened on numerous occasions, a safety valve was added. Thus the town was treated to the spectacle of enormous fountains of brown storm water jetted so high into the sky that they landed on the main road some distance away!

Marrying with Strings Attached

Superstition and marriage go hand in hand – 'something borrowed, something blue', or the bride throwing a bouquet over her shoulder for example. On Dartmoor it was the practice to sling an old boot or shoe at the departing newly weds to wish them good luck and assure them of a happy marriage. However, at Moretonhampstead, in Edwardian times, there was one occasion when this was done but, within weeks, the marriage broke down. One shoe was obviously not strong enough, so at the next wedding in the town **all** the guests armed themselves with a shoe; as the couple left for their honeymoon, a hail of shoes was targeted at their horse and carriage. Presumably they 'hot-footed' it out of town pretty darn fast!

Something Along Those Lines ...

From the relative heights of the 'Land of the Dancing Tree', runs the valley of the River Wrey. It follows a geological fault, carrying the river down to join the Bovey then on into the natural amphitheatre known as the Bovey Basin. Man has utilised this corridor for the railroad which once ran down through Lustleigh to Bovey Tracey and then to Newton Abbot.

Moretonhampstead was the rail head or terminus, lying several hundred feet above sea level. The old steam trains which chugged up this most attractive of valleys found it hard work. However, on the return journey they could hardly contain themselves as the

downward slope hastened their progress.

Now one would hardly label Moreton as a centre of nightlife – invariably its streets are as quiet as a graveyard, specially after midnight. However, in the past, when dances and balls were held in the town, people coming up the valley were restricted as to how long they could stay. Like Cinderella, they had to leave when the appointed hour was reached, only in their case it wasn't a pumpkin but the last train down the valley they had to catch! Fortunately for Bovey folk a fairy godmother provided them with one of those open wagons which could be manually slowed or stopped by applying a brake. This was attached to the last train up, then shunted into a siding for later. In the wee small hours, the party-goers would rendezvous back at the station, no doubt in high spirits, give a big heave-to and jump in to the truck for the silent but swift journey through the dead of night, down the valley. Hopefully nobody was ever strolling along the line in blissful ignorance thinking that they were totally safe as the last train had long gone ... about six hours ahead of the last wagon!

Today Moreton's trains are just a memory as the station has given way to another form of transport – the lorry. Whereas the former plied their way down the valley almost unnoticed, the lorries often cause delays on the road whose route down to Bovey Tracey could well have been designed by a drunk it is so twisty. Such is the age of progress.

Bovey Fire Engine

At about the time of the First World War there was both good news and bad news for the people of Bovey Tracey (and surrounding countryside). The good news was that this small Dartmoor borderland town had its own fire engine. The bad news was that it did not possess any horses with which to pull it! The Parish Council, in their infinite wisdom, decreed

that any residents in need of the fire engine had to take a pair of horses down to get it – and were also held responsible for taking it back afterwards. Inevitably the delay whilst arrangements were made caused many a minor flare-up to turn into a major conflagration!

The Bell Inn was a favoured location for the on duty crew to be found, being just a few doors away from the fire station. One evening, when the firemen were all well lubricated, the alarm was raised. As the crew staggered out to man the engine, one intoxicated fellow asked the landlady for a candle. When she asked why, he replied that he needed to find the fire of course, and it was dark out there!

Lustleigh Dogs and Cats and Runaway Trucks

Lustleigh was the main village on the line down the valley. Its station was used for a 1930s version of *The Hound of the Baskervilles* and it is possible that Conan Doyle knew it well as he was a regular visitor to the area.

For a while Lustleigh had a 'station cat', a friendly specimen and a familiar sight to regular passengers. Jumbo was a typical cat who led a charmed life, dicing with death on numerous occasions by dodging beneath the wheels of trains. However, he lived to a grand age and eventually died in his bed. The stationmaster decided to bury him on the platform, which he did with great ceremony. As a lasting memorial he even made a tiny headstone with this little rhyme: 'Beneath this slab and laid out flat, Lies Jumbo, once our station cat.'

Sometimes passengers waiting to board the down train to Newton would see the locomotive approach from Moreton, apply its brakes, but continue well beyond the station. The ineffective brakes on these early engines meant the passengers had to race down the the line after the train to catch it. There were no guarantees either – on one occasion some trucks were dislodged near Lustleigh and ended up at Teigngrace some five miles down the line!

An Act of God?

The River Walkham travels down the Walkham Valley to pass the Dartmoor Inn at Merrivale, a lovely pub with a welcoming atmosphere. Like all Dartmoor rivers, it rises

quickly after a storm and on one occasion an elderly man perished when trying to cross it, just up river from the pub. The inquest was held at the Dartmoor Inn and the 'crowner' (equivalent to a coroner) presided over a jury composed of moorland farmers. The foreman stated that the elderly man died by virtue of 'a visitation of the Almighty brought on by crossing the river when it was vlided' (flooded).

When is a Pub not a Pub?

When it's a cardboard cut-out! This photograph shows a set used in a film which starred Jane Seymour and Trevor Eve. If it looks vaguely familiar, it's because it's meant to be 'Jamaica Inn', a real pub on Bodmin Moor. The modern day pub on Bodmin Moor was not suitable for filming, so this authentic-looking replica was constructed on Dartmoor.

Uninformed locals at Okehampton got quite a shock as it loomed out of the moorland mist at them – they really believed that they had been pixie-led down to Cornwall!

There have been many adverts, films and television programmes filmed on Dartmoor – you can read about them in *Made in Devon*.

A Last Ditch Effort ...

The East Dart Hotel at Postbridge has had a few name changes. In the nineteenth century it was Webb's Hotel, named after its owner Captain John Webb. He passed it on to his son whose wife was a fervent teetotaller. She did her best to teach her husband the error of his ways, but he would contrive to escape her nagging about the evils of the Demon drink by seeking sanctuary at the local chapel. However one Sunday, at Evensong, the preacher delivered a stinging, probably pointed, sermon on alcohol. It was all too much for the young landlord; he promptly went home, took every bottle of liquor from his inn and emptied the lot into a ditch on the opposite side of the road. It is said that at about 3 a.m. each day, a bloodhound approaches from the Moretonhampstead direction, stops at the ditch and laps up the dregs of alcohol. Somewhat aptly the inn's other past names include 'The Temperance Inn' and 'The Greyhound'.

Shhhh!

There once was an inn called the Half Moon, which was situated at Manaton, well up the road from the present Kes Tor Inn, close to the parish church. It was described as a homely place and its 'fayre' included cakes and cheese. Up until its closure in 1920, these undoubted attractions drew all manner of folk to it. But not everyone wanted to be seen patronising such premises so they used a quiet, green path leading from the outer margins of the community almost up to the pub's door. This path was so well used by thirsty/well lubricated locals (depending on which way the 'tide' was flowing) that it was given the name of Slinker's Lane!

Dartmoor's Pink Elephants

Some old maps will show a country pub at Horndon, formerly a farmhouse, as The New Inn. Today it trades under the much more unusual name of The Elephant's Nest, a strange name because elephants do not make nests, nor do they frequent the north western side of Dartmoor (although of course it is not too far from the nearest trunk road!).

How and why then did this extremely popular inn get its name? Well, landlords come in all shapes and sizes but at this pub the landlord was definitely 'outsize' – a giant who was as round as he was tall. To save himself from even the slightest form of physical exercise, a custom-made stool was designed for the purpose of accommodating his ample and excessive frame. Thus, once ensconced, he could direct operations with the least possible exertion. One day, a customer, observing this spectacle, boldly proclaimed that this vast vision reminded him of an elephant sat on a nest. The landlord laughed at the comment, and the inn duly changed its name.

Widecombe in the Moor

No book about Dartmoor is complete without some reference to its most famous village, Widecombe-in-the-Moor. It is so well known that people the world over will be familiar with its song which features Bill Brewer, Jan Stewer, Peter Gurney, Peter Davy, Dan'l Whiddon, Harry Hawk, old Uncle Tom Cobley and all. Of course it is this wonderful publicity which has put this tiny village well and truly on the map. (The Beatles had obviously heard of it for, on their legendary *Magical Mystery Tour,* they tried to visit this moorland settlement, but their direction of approach was the wrong one and they were thwarted by a too-narrow granite bridge.)

Although most people can sing at least a few lines of the song, there are precious few visitors who know from where these chaotic characters originated, or by which route they entered 'town', or even if they ever truly existed.

It is believed that the song is a distortion or exaggeration of the truth, involving some folk from an area many miles to the north. Sticklepath certainly had a mill owner called Tom Pearce, and all the other names are local names. Further north still is the tiny hilltop village of Spreyton. It is a one-horse town (but not the famous grey mare). Here the names of many cottages and the inn reflect the connection, but only a trickle of pilgrims come to pay homage to the legend.

Tom Cobley lived at Spreyton until his death in about 1800. He was an 'ancient' and well-to-do, but the grave in the churchyard is that of his nephew, the recipient of the great man's wealth. The nephew was chosen as heir in favour of Tom Cobley's own son, who was too much of a womaniser!

Spreyton has a mortal population of only 300, but ghosts aplenty. Sightings in the past

WIDECOMBE VILLAGE.

include a kneeling boy by a bedside at the Vicarage, a little boy in blue, an old lady searching for her son, yet another old lady in black looking for her money, and if you throw in, for good measure, the old grey mare with Tom atop it, riding off to the moors in order to become immortalised in a folk song, then you have a village with definitely more spooks than tourists!

The song itself is a traditional one which has been sung in some strange languages (there is even a Japanese version!) and places. To have witnessed the Devonshire Regiment sing it with pride as they marched into battle in the Boer War, in 1899, must have been a particularly moving and stirring sight. Various Victorians wrote down the song but the Reverend Sabine Baring-Gould, famous in his own rights, popularised it in 1891 by including it in his *Songs of the West*. Coincidentally this was the year of the blizzard when such a journey would have been even more of an adventure – the walk from Spreyton to Widecombe, with careful route planning, can be an enjoyable, but tiring, twenty miles romp in the best of conditions. The song has been sung by no less a celebrity than the famous Scottish music-hall entertainer Sir Harry Lauder (1870–1950) who visited Widecombe in the Moor and sang on the village green.

A Typical Visit to Widecombe

Visitors to Widecombe come in all shapes and sizes! Having reached the safety and civilisation of Widecombe's main car park, their mission to visit the shrine of Tom Cobley is well under way. Out comes the compact cameras (part of the survival kit for visitors), ready for the obligatory photograph of the village sign with its Tom Cobley and drunken crew frozen in stone. The attraction of this monument lies in its ideal height to stand behind/beside/between (depending of numbers in the picture) to proudly proclaim the visit authentic.

When the photo-call is over it is time to move on to the church of St Pancras – the Cathedral of the Moor. Not many will persevere in trying to decipher the story of how the church was struck by lightning on 21 October 1638 as the f's and s's cause much difficulty.

Next on the itinerary are the gift shops. It is highly probable that something bearing an image of Tom Cobley and Co. will be purchased, if only a postcard, a mug, a pen or a teatowel.

Then the final move is to the tea rooms, where the smartly uniformed staff have clocked up years of serving real Devonshire cream teas, followed by reboarding the coach to return to the holiday accommodation. That's Dartmoor 'done', tomorrow it's Exeter ...

Dartmoor Prison – (Get out of that!)

Austere, bleak, windswept and God-forsaken are simply a selection of the many words or terms used to describe Dartmoor Prison. In fact it is so far removed from a 'des. res.' that a high proportion of its inmates, dating back to Napoleonic War times, have given much thought to the possibilities of escaping, despite the inclement climate and the inhospitable nature of the surrounding moorlands.

In its early days, when the prison was a war depot for prisoners of war rather than criminals, it held a handsome young French sailor who used his undoubted Gallic charm to strike up a very friendly relationship with a local girl. One warm, fine day he persuaded her to remove all her clothes ... whereupon he promptly donned them himself, bid her 'adieu', and made good his escape. He was not heard of again!

Another Frenchman, Louis Vanhille, attempted a similar deception. His young lady, Fanny Tyeth, persuaded a Tavistock girl to smuggle a waggoner's costume to him, but his freedom lasted only a year having got as far as Jamaica before being returned to Chatham.

The most ingenious breakout implemented by the French was plotted by Monsieurs Sanbot and Routier. They wrote a little play called *Captain Colonne et sa Dame* about the officer in charge of the garrison and his good lady wife. Highly flattered, the Captain loaned them one of his uniforms and his wife also obliged with one of her dresses, to aid

authenticity. The play was in three acts and was met with generous applause at the end of the first one. However, as the interval became suspiciously long, Captain Colonne went to investigate the delay. He was amazed and aghast to discover that the two leading actors had marched arm in arm right out of the gateway. Insult was then added to injury when the guard refused to let the real Captain and his wife leave – on account that they had already gone! Sanbot and Routier deservedly made it back to France.

Naturally a much more rigid and restricted regime had to be applied when it became a criminal prison in the mid nineteenth century, and would-be escapees had to really apply themselves to the task in hand. But many of the men who have ended up in Dartmoor Gaol are natural con men, masters of deception. Take the case of a prisoner, in April 1928, who made a skeleton key. This gave him access to a workshop where he acquired the necessary wherewithal to scale the wall. Quickly he then broke into a priest's house and, disguised as Father Finnegan, he used the priest's car to leave town. He even had the audacity to wave at people he passed, including a policeman who politely saluted him! 'Father Finnegan' enjoyed two days of freedom before being arrested at Paignton.

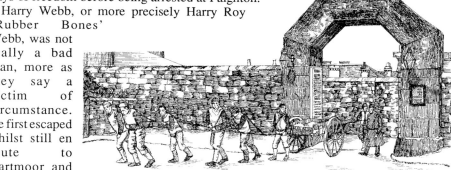

Harry Webb, or more precisely Harry Roy 'Rubber Bones' Webb, was not really a bad man, more as they say a victim of circumstance. He first escaped whilst still en route to Dartmoor and endured a couple of terrible days wandering around in the wilderness. The Tavistock constabulary, on recapturing him, treated him so humanely that he always remembered and talked of their kindness.

In Dartmoor his habitual desire to escape, without really anywhere to go, manifested itself in a classic text book escape bid. Because of his previous history of going walkabout, maximum surveillance of his activities was arranged. However, he managed to conceal a needle at the end of every shift that he worked. He then made a dummy of himself which he attached to a string, so that when the warden peeped in, at fifteen minute intervals, he could jiggle it enough to simulate a sleeping movement. Cleverly he knew of the warden's approach as a strategically placed bowl of water would be disturbed by the approaching footsteps. In the meantime he painstakingly used the needles to chip away at the floor towards the system of ventilation pipes running along beneath.

He carefully chose the optimum time of the wee small hours of a Sunday morning to crawl along the shaft. It had to be a wet and windy night to mask any sounds that he might make. With this as cover he broke into a workshop and took enough protective clothing to see him on his way to Brentor Station, a straight line distance of about nine miles. He impersonated a railway employee and managed to get a journey to Exeter. From here he opted to use road transport by hitch-hiking all the way to London.

However, his resourcefulness was wasted as there was nobody on the 'outside' to help him and he was soon returned to Princetown.

The Mad Axeman

Frank Mitchell's exploits at Dartmoor Gaol are legendary. Whilst at the prison his 'persuasive' personality is believed to have won him privileges and perks, although if truth be known his luxurious lifestyle was probably grossly exaggerated. His nickname – 'The Mad Axeman' – was, however, justified as his life sentence was received for

threatening two people with one. He escaped whilst working near Bagga Tor on 12 December 1966 – which surprised many folk as they felt that he had mellowed considerably whilst there. Because of his past history of violence, and his close associations with 'Gangland', a massive hunt was organised. Even the Royal Marines were called in to help hunt for 'The Mad Axeman'. But despite all the efforts made to find him, nothing materialised other than his prison clothing, which was found near Crockernwell on the A30 between Exeter and Okehampton, with a twelve inch-long broad-bladed knife. He was never found and it is unknown whether his is alive and well living in peaceful exile or was he, as many believe, lured out of prison to be murdered in order to silence him for all time?

Not Too Far from the Madding Crowd!

The French prisoners of war held at Princetown during the Napoleonic Wars (1793–1815) came from across the complete spectrum of social classes, ranging from the dregs of society, called 'Les Romans' to the aristocrats who were referred to as 'Les Lords'. However the soldiers of officer status were treated very differently, being farmed out to 'parole' towns like Tavistock, Moretonhampstead, Tiverton, Crediton and Ashburton

(where there is a grave to a young French officer, François Guidon, who died at the tender age of twenty two). Most of these men were billeted with traders in the town and, although some people were rude and abusive to them, despite a law against it, most folk just went about their business, soon becoming accustomed to seeing them around. Many French men even stayed on afterwards to marry local girls.

Naturally there were restrictions on their freedom, one of them resulting in an enterprising and amusing deed. To a degree, in the daylight hours, the French could do what they liked. However, a regulation clearly stipulated that nobody was to go further than one mile away from the town. To ensure the boundaries were clear, milestones were placed on all roads leading from the towns.

There were seven roads which led away from Ashburton, but despite the many different directions the Frenchmen could choose for variety, each time they tried to head south-east towards Broadhempston, their enjoyment was diminished because the milestone was just before a sharp bend. Their curiosity knew no bounds. Not wishing to break the conditions of parole, they could not go beyond the milestone. Then they devised a cunning plan. They were young, fit, healthy and strong. All they had to do was to lift the milestone and hump it around the bend. This they did – and there it remains to this day!

At Moretonhampstead, at one time or another, there were 379 French prisoners of war. The most celebrated was Rochambeau who had been Commander-in-Chief at San Domingo. He was a fervent nationalist who amused the people of Moreton every time he received news of a French victory, for he would don full military uniform and, wearing all his medals proudly, parade through the town. With his chest fully expanded, his shoulders stiff and pinned back, he would march up and down for hours at a time. Rochambeau was much respected but in 1811 he was returned to combat and was slain some two years later at Leipzig.

Only Home Matches

Dartmoor Prison has witnessed its lighter moments ...

A charity soccer match was organised between the prison and a local radio station. As the latter doesn't have its own pitch, it was rather opportune that the prison team were confined to playing at 'home'.

It was a winter Sunday when the only thing moving in the main street was a hurricane. To describe Princetown that day as a ghost town might be apt, but no self-respecting ghost would have ventured out in such appalling conditions. The only concession yielded by the weather was that the great wind was a dry one.

There were no signs of life anywhere as the 'visitors' arrived, so one member took the initiative and knocked heavily on the prison doors. Confronted with an enormous prison

officer, he enquired 'Please could the football team come out to play?'

Emerging from the unheated sports hall changing rooms, the team was met by the sight of a pitch which was rutted like the craters of the moon, whilst the Siberian-like wind bore little 'glasnost' as it ripped mercilessly from end to end.

There was no way of telling whether the opposition was made up of officers or inmates, as in their soccer gear they all looked alike. It was, however, presumed that the referee was a prison employee and not someone doing time for bribery and corruption!

The game was one of two halves (to quote a tried and trusted expression). Depending on which you side you were on, in the first half one team exerted all their efforts in trying to inch forward only to be blown back, whilst the other had to apply the brakes to avoid being blown down the pitch and into the prison's perimeter fence (and vice versa). Nature even dictated the result – which was 2-2 – with the wind scoring all four goals!

Throughout the game the wind persistently blew the ball down a bank at the far end of the pitch. Unlike most football matches which usually have at least a handful of willing 'retrievers' to fetch the ball, this game had no supporters other than a few wives and girlfriends who had no intention of leaving the comparative warmth of their cars to fetch a muddy football! So when the ball disappeared over the bank for the umpteenth time, one of the opposition suggested that they let it roll down yet another bank, and then he would make good his getaway! This player was presumed to be an inmate and not a warder, but who knows?

Princetown Airport?

Being the 'highest' town in Devon, Princetown is fully exposed to the worst of any bad weather which assaults the South-west. Its rainfall figures are horrendous, and when the wind whistles it can seem very much like the most God-forsaken spot in Devon. At such times it is prone to lose its electricity supply, but fortunately for the residents of this bleak, moorland settlement, it has a most unusual back-up ...

Since 1959 a Bristol Britannia airliner's engine has filled the role of emergency generator. It has complete automatic remote control which will start it up immediately there is an emergency. Although there have been similar installations of other aircraft engines at Lynton in North Devon, Mevagissey in Cornwall and Porlock in Somerset, Princetown can claim the honour of being the first. It's appropriate that an engine which has flown hundreds of thousands of miles should be grounded at a place where the weather is often so bad that it would be difficult to take off anyway. Perhaps too it serves as a reminder to residents that it is safe to leave their 'landing lights' on when the electricity goes off, as it won't be too long before it comes back on again.

England's Highest Railway Line

You could once go all the way up to Princetown by rail. It was the highest station in England and close scrutiny of the ordnance survey map shows that the engineers had to resort to great sweeps around each hillside. The straight line distance from Yelverton to Princetown was about half that taken by the train; for ten and half miles it snaked its way tortuously and slowly upwards.

For many years it had two regular Princetown-based drivers. One of them lived for his night of 'whist' so if he was on

duty there was never any worry that the train would be late or delayed as every bit of power was channelled into getting to Princetown on time!

On arrival the engine was placed in a snug little shed. Care of the carriages extended to placing a sign on them which said 'Return to Princetown' should they ever wander off into the gloom of a misty moor.

Generally the line was casual in the way it was run. It was not unusual for trains to stop between halts for the convenience of its regular passengers. There were four official stops between Yelverton and Princetown: Dousland, a staffed station, Burrator, Ingra Tor and King Tor, all unmanned halts.

Technically trains which ran from Yelverton to Princetown were 'down' trains – a bit daft as the line ran continuously uphill all the way to Princetown! However that was only one idiosyncrasy of a line that possessed many. At Dousland the signal box was called Dousland Barn. The signalman had to board Princetown-bound trains and travel as far as the next level crossing. Here he would alight, open the crossing gates, let the train through, re-close the gates and then trudge back along the line to Dousland!

The lonely Ingra Tor Halt was noted for an unusual sign which warned alighting passengers with dogs, of the possible presence of snakes. (Dogs run across the moor with their noses to the ground and adders take the intrusion quite personally.) The sign has been kept, restored, and is now in a museum collection at Saltram House, Plymouth.

The station master at Princetown was Charlie Windsor. When he relinquished the post it was taken on by his son, also Charlie Windsor. This is particularly befitting of a station in a largely Duchy owned landscape, in a town named after a Prince. Not to be outdone, Lustleigh, on eastern Dartmoor, has the Tudor Memorial Cross on its small village green which is in memory of the rector who served the parish from 1888 to 1904 – his name was Henry Tudor!

You Dirty Rat!

In the borderland towns of Dartmoor there are many examples of how the moor's fast flowing rivers were harnessed for their power. In some cases there are mill wheels still in place with examples at Bovey Tracey, Okehampton and Sticklepath. The principal was simple – a small watercourse, called a leat, was taken from the river and thus carried the waters to the waterwheel. The favourite type of wheel was the overshot, where the water went over the top of the wheel to maximise the power. In turn the rotating wheel turned a gear system that operated the mill's machinery. When the mill needed to close down, a sluice gate would stop the water supply – simple but pure genius. Alas at Bickington corn mill, on the River Lemon in 1881, things did not go quite to plan.

At the end of the day the sluice gates were closed and tied up and the millers went home. That night some rats were feeling a bit peckish and gnawed their way through the cord securing the sluice gates. Thus the gates opened, letting the water run along the leat and turn the waterwheel. This in turn worked the gear system which, in this case, operated two enormous grind stones. Naturally, as there was no corn between the two stones, great sparks flew out. The mill was largely constructed of timber so soon burnt down to the ground. This is one of the few situations where water actually started a fire rather than put it out!

Bringing the House Down

Ilsington is usually a quiet village, located just over a mile from Haytor Rocks. Being away from any major roads it retains a calm, civilised atmosphere. However, in 1639 it was the scene of a most bizarre occurrence.

A small room built above the lich gate of the parish church of St Michael was used as the village school, which consisted twenty nine pupils and a master. On 17 September there were a dozen boys away, whilst the rest of the school were busily engaged in their studies. At around 11 a.m. a local lady passed through the lich gate on her way towards the church. The gate was heavy so she let go of it almost at its widest extent. The speed of the swing combined with the weight created a tremendous impact on the structure of the Lich Gate: the south wall collapsed; the roof fell in; and all the walls crashed about the ears of the startled scholars. Four pupils were knocked into the churchyard, another was dispatched into the street only to be immediately buried beneath a pile of

rubble, whilst another was trapped beneath the room. The ones who had escaped with minor injuries, set about rescuing those who had been less fortunate. Miraculously nobody was inflicted with too serious an injury and everyone gave thanks for their deliverance.

At Chagford there was a similar disaster in 1617 when the court house fell down whilst a meeting was taking place in an upper room. Here, though, the assembled group were less fortunate and ten people were killed.

I Name this Stone

The Rev. Edward Atkyns Bray was quite a character, a romantic, Victorian eccentric in love with poetry, literature and Dartmoor. His wife was the author of books about the area and shared his passion for the written word.

They inherited an area of land near Two Bridges, which included the lower part of the unromantic sounding Cowsic Valley, a place where Edward loved to explore. He knew every pool and stickle and whilst there decided to dedicate certain boulders to poets. Thus armed with a pot of paint and a brush he would daub various rocks with dedications. Next, which some still regard as desecration, he would hire a man to chisel the dedication into the rocks as a more lasting message. Edward thought that his actions brought the valley to life, and lines from poems with dedications like 'To Milton' and 'To Shakespeare' were numerous.

Nature's agents of erosion have worn down his literary appendages but mention of it is enough to raise the blood pressure of preservationists who are opposed to anything of this sort on Dartmoor being done again.

Dartmoor's Llamas

One grey, misty day, a group of French students, staying in Exeter, were on a day trip to Dartmoor. A suitable guide (guess who?) was hired, and countless questions, posed in sentences of broken English, were handled with consummate ease – until the coach approached Two Bridges. Slipping back into their native tongue, amidst much excitement and chatter, a spokesperson was appointed to ask the 64,000 dollar question: 'Chips, Chips, 'ow you call these animals? They are llamas, no?' Of course llamas are not an indigenous species to Dartmoor so without glancing out of the window they were told 'They're sheep' (wrong), 'Well goats then' (wrong), 'Must be ponies' (wrong again). So what did our

intrepid guide see when he deigned to look out the window? Correct – llamas! In fact quite a few llamas peered over the wall, out of the mist, as the coach crawled by at about five miles per hour.

It transpired that the people who owned the hotel at that time had previously owned the Farway Country Park in East Devon and on selling up had decided to take the llamas with them to Dartmoor. So be advised, if someone asks you to identify an impossibility, take a good look first!

Signs of the Times

Around the roads of Dartmoor there have been, and still are, examples of unusual cautions or requests.

Between Postbridge and Widecombe, on one of those twisting, turning back lanes, in the late 1940s a sign on a gate stated 'Please shut the gate. Your meat rations will stray.'

The sign shown here appeared beside the road from Chagford to Scorhill near Gidleigh. It is included in this book by popular demand as whenever it is shown as a colour slide, at talks to various groups throughout the county, it never fails to raise a smile. Each person no doubt conjures up their own mental image of what this 'deaf old dog' may be like. Presumably it does refer to a member of the canine variety.

Clocking Out

Lydford is the biggest parish in England, yet one of the most sparsely populated as it takes in land which is in the Forest of Dartmoor, an area of bleak, open moorland. An ancient track, sometimes referred to as 'The Way of the Dead' but named on maps as 'The Lich Way' traverses this wilderness. For centuries funeral processions made their way to Lydford's Church. Today they make the journey by road to take their dearly departed to their final resting places below Dartmoor's hills.

One grave in Lydford has a quite extraordinary epitaph; it marks the final resting place of George Routleigh who, for years, was the local watchmaker. Lovers of puns will find it amusing and appropriate for it says: 'Here lies in a horizontal position, the outward case of George Routleigh, Watchmaker, whose abilities in that line were an honour to his profession. Integrity was the main spring and prudence the regulator of all the actions of his life. Humane, generous and liberal, his hand never stopped till he had relieved distress. So nicely regulated were all his motions that he never went wrong except when set agoing by people who did not know his key. Even then he was easily set aright. He had the art of disposing of his time so well that his hours glided away in one continual round of pleasure and delight till an unlucky minute put a period to his existence. He departed this life November 14, 1802 aged 57. Wound up in hope of being taken in hand by his Maker and of being thoroughly cleaned and repaired and set agoing in the world to come.'

Some five miles to the south lies the even quieter village of Peter Tavy. The Rector, Richard Eveleigh, and his wife had miserable luck in trying to rear children. They were blessed with five daughters but none of them survived for more than a year. The inscription on a wall in the church says 'They breathed awhile and looked the world about, And, like newly-lighted candles, soon went out.'

Our Lovely Little Lilly

Shipley Bridge, three miles to the north of South Brent, is a beauty spot which is busy even on dull week days. The track that runs up the valley is the perfect corridor for those who want access to great moorland scenery. A little way up the road a gateway is reached, marking the entrance to the former Brentmoor House.

Within the grounds on the left hand side is a memorial to Margaret Meynell who was affectionately known as 'Lilly' to members of her family. This touching little monument is well above head height and is so easily missed by the thousands who stroll just yards away from it as they head towards the Avon Dam.

To take a picture is difficult, even with the correct lens, as the temptation is to edge back those few precious inches to frame the picture; alas the little rocky ledge on which it is located does not permit this. However, the inscription says: ' My lovely little Lilly, thou wert gathered very soon in the fresh and dewy morning, not in the glare of noon. The Saviour sent his angels to bear thee hence, my own. And they'll plant thee in that garden where decay is never known.

The Dreamer who Built a Chapel and a Church

Keble is an unusual Christian name and Keble Martin was a fairly unusual young man of strong Christian convictions. As a youngster he would spend his holidays on Dartmoor following a great number of outdoor pursuits and, at the same time, he developed an interest in his natural surroundings. In the later years of his life this enthusiasm was reflected in his book *Concise British Flora*.

His Dartmoor nights were spent under canvas beneath starry skies. Each year, for ten consecutive summers 1904–1914, the Martin family camped at Huntingdon Warren about a mile north west of the Avon Dam now stands. In order to continue their worship, Keble and his brother Jack built their own (roofless) chapel, the ruins of which still remain today. The Duchy of Cornwall gave them permission to shoot rabbits and fish for trout in the cool, clean waters of the Avon where they would also bathe for endless hours.

However there were religious tasks to perform; a baby born at Huntingdon Warren Farm, in 1904, needed to be baptised so they performed the service on behalf of the Vicar of Lydford, the parish in which they were camped. (Lydford church, as the crow flies, was thirteen miles distant over some of the wettest and wildest parts of the Dartmoor wilderness – a long way to go to church, especially on foot.)

Keble was to continue his career in the church and became Rector of Coffinswell, a small village tucked away in a quiet backwater a few miles from Newton Abbot. His job included the district of Milber which was expanding so quickly that it was in great need of its own church. One night Keble had such a vivid dream that, over his early morning cuppa, he sketched down his 'vision' for a new church. With the help of his architect brother the church came into being, but the building begun in 1935 was not completed until 1963. It is an elaborate structure which is by sheer coincidence 1,000 inches tall, 1,000 inches wide (overall) and 1,000 inches long (overall). From it Keble Martin's beloved Dartmoor can just about be seen.

The Swashbuckling Sermon

If you have ever endured a long and tedious sermon you may feel some sympathy for the mid-nineteenth-century clerk of Lustleigh church. The vicar had got himself into a local row so each service was conducted by a visiting speaker. One of them was an enthusiastic type who gesticulated wildly. Just as the clerk had dropped off for his customary forty winks, the speaker gave a large sweep of his arms, causing all manner of church furniture to be dispatched in all directions – glasses, candles and even a cushion. The poor clerk must have got quite a shock as the latter landed on his slumbering head, but instinctively he was alert and loudly proclaimed, 'Amen'.

Off the Peg

Cornwood is a sleepy village on the road from Ivybridge to Yelverton. Its peace was once shattered by an argument which got out of all proportion. A man called Savery was caught fighting in Cornwood churchyard. His punishment was to publicly beg pardon from Sir John Rogers, an act which he grudgingly carried out on St Bartholomew's Day in 1734. Feeling somewhat humiliated, he vowed to get his revenge on Sir John.

At the church he cut off the pegs on which Sir John and his family hung their garments. Arriving at church early for the service, Savery eagerly awaited the reaction of Sir John. All went to plan for the family, thwarted by the missing pegs, put their outer garments over the parclose screen. Savery knew this was an ecclesiastical misdemeanour and promptly prosecuted Sir John and family at the Court of Delegates in Totnes. However the prosecution backfired on him and he, in turn, was fined £300 – quite a fortune in the eighteenth century – which must have brought him down a peg or two!

How Time Flies ...

In the days when most country people didn't own a watch, and radio ownership was far less common, there was great dependence on church clocks for telling the time. So if the clock was wrong, then problems would arise.

At Drewsteignton, during the war, Tom Ashplant was on Home Guard duty at the top of the church tower, a generally inactive affair apart from climbing and descending the stairs. He was a big man and to lighten his load, on the downward journey after finishing his watch, he would remove his great overcoat and lob it down onto the footpath below. Unfortunately, one early and windy morning, this energy-conserving exploit misfired. Instead of falling to earth, the coat hooked over the minute hand on the clock, which had reached the hour, and the coat's weight whipped it instantly around to half past. Time, in sleepy Drewsteignton, had jumped from 6.00 a.m. to 6.30 a.m, at a stroke. The offending garment then followed the law of gravity, leaving the church clock to continue some thirty minutes ahead of schedule.

There followed considerable confusion; those with wirelesses were being told it was one time, whilst the church clock, which was 'gospel' and therefore must be correct, said something quite different. Tom owned up to the Rector and never again dared repeat his coat throwing act.

The Nutcrackers

It usually raises a smile (or brings tears to the eyes) whenever the celebrated old logan stone called The Nutcrackers is mentioned. This logan stone was once a feature of Lustleigh Cleave. A logan stone is a rocking stone, delicately balanced so that the slightest weight could move, in the case, a rock of some eight to ten tons; the logan would rock or 'log' to and fro. This one, as its name implies, was used by villagers for crushing their nuts – at Christmas time usually.

Sadly, one morning in May 1950 it was noticed that the stone had toppled off its perch. In its forty feet fall it had split but, as it was deemed such an important feature, 'Operation Nutcracker' was launched the following month. Major E.H. Graham brought forty soldiers from Plymouth together with a winch weighing half a ton. For two long days they tried to engineer the rock back to its original resting place but the shape, location and volume of the rock defeated them. One local wag said that it was 'too tough a nut for them to crack'. After some 1200 man hours spent on the salvage operation, the rock suddenly broke free of the tackle holding it and plunged a further hundred feet down the hillside. In the process, watched by many villagers, the rock kicked up a thick cloud of sulphurous smoke.

The logan stone is now just a memory, shattered into fragments over the hillside and the villagers are left to find more conventional ways to crack their nuts.

Pixie Cave

The ring of tors around the man-made lake of Burrator Reservoir is a series of granite citadels, a wonderful backcloth to a spectacular scene. Sheepstor is one of the rockiest of them all and its hillsides are awash with great accumulations of moorstone. One small conglomeration has acquired the title 'Pixie-cave' because the rocks have formed a large chamber.

Before the Meavy Valley was dammed to create the reservoir, a family called Elford lived at Longstone Manor. In the English Civil War they were fervent Royalists. One of the Elford family became the target of Cromwell's troops and, chased by them, he sought refuge in this cave. Although they searched the hillside they didn't find his hidey-hole. Safe within, he amused himself by engraving the side of the cave with drawings until it was safe to emerge and fight for another day.

At one time it was estimated that it could hold a number of people, but Dartmoor expert, William Crossing, considered that by 1909 it had become unsafe and recommended walkers to exercise care.

Hinkypunks

Who were the original settlers of Dartmoor? Historians will tell you that Stone-age man was first but legend has it that the first inhabitants were called 'Hinkypunks'. They knew the terrain well so would act as guides for travellers across the moor. But there were two distinct varieties: the good ones who would who ensure their charges had a dry, safe passage; and the bad ones who would deliberately lead people into the muckiest mires, then stand to watch and gloat as they struggled. Both types of Hinkypunk had a distinct appearance with only one arm and a leg, and they possessed grotesque goblinesque faces. So if you encounter one near Raybarrow Pool, Gidleigh Common Mire or at Foxtor Mires, try to ascertain whether this is a descendant of a 'good' ancient Hinkypunk or a 'bad' one – your safety might depend on it!

Galsworthy's Dartmoor Saga

Just up the road from Becky Falls is the small village of Manaton, a good example of what geographers call a disseminated settlement, or more simply a scattered village. It is possibly this that led to the demise of its pub, the Half Moon, whose fortunes waxed and waned before it finally closed.

Now the nearest place of refreshment is at the headquarters of the MCC down at nearby Water. By MCC they mean the Manaton Cricket Club and at one time it had a very famous player. Unfortunately his prowess was not as a cricketer, but as a playwright for he was John Galsworthy, author of the *Forsyte Saga* and winner of the Nobel Prize for Literature in 1932. It is believed that in his seventeen seasons as an MCC player he failed to trouble the scorers. On the one occasion he claimed to put bat to ball for a boundary, the official scorer instead recorded leg byes. It is therefore obvious that his manuscripts were considerably longer than his innings!

In the late 1960s R.F. Delderfield, author of such novels as *A Horseman Riding By,* unveiled a plaque on the verandah of Wingstone Farm, a place where so many of Galsworthy's characters were created.

A Cross Vicar

For reasons best known to early Victorian Manatonians, when they carried a body for burial to Manaton's churchyard, they ritualistically paraded the coffin thrice times around a cross. The Rev J.C. Carwithen was determined to stop this practice but his appeals and edicts fell on deaf ears. So frustrated was he that it is believed he was responsible for the removal of the cross. A long search, spanning more than three score years, ensued until, at last, in 1911 the long lost cross was discovered near a small stream just under a quarter of a mile from the church. It was duly exhumed and ensconced once more in its rightful

position. Alas some twenty six years later it was declared that there was no way that this could have been the original cross for it was too basic in every detail. The search goes on – so if you stumble across a substantial granite cross, please let them know.

Tinners and Sinners

To an outsider most of Dartmoor's hundreds of tors probably look the same, but those who are familiar with this granite landscape will appreciate all manner of differences from location to shape and size. There is even a variation in colour from the greyest mass of Haytor through to the reddishness of outcrops like Trowlesworthy Tors. They are all very different and some have been known to serve some unusual purposes.

Crockern Tor is beside the main road over the moor from Moreton to Princetown, not far from the junction at Two Bridges of the road that runs from Ashburton across to Tavistock. From about 1494 this tor was used as a regular meeting place for Parliament. This was not the madcap assembly of MP normally associated with Westminster, but the ninety six representatives of the tinners' or Stannary Parliament. This word derives from the Latin word for tin, stannum, and those scholarly types who are familiar with symbols and abbreviations will know that tin's abbreviation is Sn!

Originally the tinners' parliament represented both Devon and Cornwall's tin mines and they met on Hingston Down near Kit Hill just on the Cornish side of the River Tamar. However it was agreed that the Cornish would go their own way and the Devonshire men were left to find another venue.

As the four tin towns, Ashburton, Chagford, Plympton and Tavistock were at different corners of the moor, a central rendezvous was required and Crockern Tor was it. As the crow flies Tavistock was marginally the closest at eight and a quarter miles, Chagford just under nine miles, Ashburton just over nine miles, whilst poor old Plympton's twenty four representatives had a really rugged ramble of about thirteen miles. Apart from being ideally located near to important tracks across the moor, it was also regarded as the most central tor on Dartmoor, eleven yards off centre north to south and sixty six yards off centre east to west (1899 calculation).

In addition to the tor the tinners had a Stannary prison at Lydford on the north western side of the moor. It was a reflection of the powers and importance of the tinners, for some of the justice meted out was harsh in the extreme. A well-known rhyme, which has many variations, suggests that the accused was often executed before his trial! A large hill, a few miles above Lydford, bears the name of Gibbet Hill.

In the time of Henry VIII, the MP for Plympton, Richard Strode, introduced a Bill to Parliament (the London one) to prevent harbours being silted up. Tinners disturbing the land on the moor were causing river estuaries to become shallow as a result of accumulations of silt, brought down by swift flowing Dartmoor rivers, which settled in

the slow moving estuarine waters. This immediately brought him into direct conflict with the tinners. They summoned him to appear before them on Crockern Tor and, having refused to attend, they tried and fined him in his absence. He promptly refused to pay. He was seized and duly incarcerated in the deep, dark, damp dungeon at Lydford. Richard Strode languished there for some weeks until a £100 bond was placed with the Deputy Warden of the Stannaries and he was released.

Strode's Act was passed, and along with it went many of the privileges afforded to the tinners. The damage done to their cause was considerable and, as new sources of tin were constantly being discovered, the tin industry in Devon diminished.

The last meeting held on Crockern Tor was in 1749. It is believed that the great, natural granite table that the 'stannators' sat around was removed to Dunnabridge, two miles ESE of Crockern Tor, but there is no proof of this.

Later tin mining on the moor was sporadic. Included here is a picture taken in the vicinity of the famous Warren House Inn. Until the advent of the Second World War, a few tons of tin ore were sent to South Wales. Today the underground network of adits, shafts and passages remain undisturbed, apart from the waters which drain through an all pervading darkness.

Knockers and Knackers

Mary Tavy is a small village on the north side of the Tavy Valley on the western side of Dartmoor. The main road from Okehampton to Tavistock passes through it, as do most of the motorists that use this highway. If they stopped awhile to explore the vicinity they would discover a network of quiet lanes and some sparkling scenery. And if they were very observant they would soon discover that Mary Tavy was once a busy mining area. There are all the visible clues with spoil heaps and other industrial archaeological paraphernalia littering the landscape.

The most important concern, in this vicinity, was Wheal Friendship ('wheal' is a Celtic term meaning mine). More than 150,000 tons of copper ore was extracted in its heyday era between 1800–1885. There were many other smaller ventures like Devon United Mines, Wheal Betsy, North Betsy and Wheal Jewell all in easy walking distance. Today there is a growing interest in industrial archaeology, many people claim such relics are as much a part of our heritage as stately homes (though not quite as comfortable).

For those who look for human interest, these stark, generally untidy, remains were the workplace of some real characters. The mine captains, with their fine impressive moustaches, and the strong, strapping workers, were surprisingly superstitious. They believed in little creatures called, so it is said, 'knockers' or 'knackers'. These were cave pixies, rarely seen but oftimes heard. In exchange for titbits of food left for them, they would warn of imminent cave-ins so that the miners had a few precious moments to seek a safer position.

Above Mary Tavy is what locals will call a 'gert' hill (meaning a great, or long, hill). Those who scale the steep slopes of Gibbet Hill might find a stronger word! From its name it was obviously a place of execution by hanging, but it is believed that at one time it was also a site for more lingering deaths. Near the former gate to Blackdown, a common name for the heights in these parts, there was an iron cage where highwaymen were incarcerated and left to die as a warning to others. The gate to the down was called 'iron cage gate'.

Boliver

The A38 from Exeter to Plymouth (and beyond) is often taken for granted but the road holds many surprises and a few secrets. How many people ever realise that on this stretch the road is actually built on top of two different railway routes? For about a mile from below Chudleigh, towards Heathfield, the road sits on top of the Teign Valley Railway line, whilst between Ashburton and Buckfastleigh station (Dart Valley Railway) the dual carriageway sits on top of the line which ran down to Totnes.

Ashburton was the terminus of the line, and the ride down first the Ashburn Valley and then the Dart Valley was by courtesy of a little steam train which so won the hearts of local people that it was given the fond nickname of *Bolivar*. There was once a young lady who acquired a position as a teacher in Totnes. The nine mile journey was no problem as there were four trains each way, every day. Like many others she became fascinated with Bolivar, so much so that she plucked up the courage to ask the driver if she could ride on the footplate with him. He, of course, refused but, after politely persisting on numerous occasions, he eventually consented. Every time it was quiet she would climb on board to assist. She got to know the workings of *Bolivar* so well that eventually she was allowed to drive the train home herself, a task she thoroughly enjoyed. She must have been quite a lady as she was a Portreeve of Ashburton and also earnt herself an MBE.

A Spot of Bother?

Everyone has a threshold of tolerance, a breaking point where rational behaviour is temporarily put aside. A Tavistock man, Alfie Jordan, who lived at the workhouse in the town, would earn himself a little pocket money by pushing a wheelchair-bound man about the town. Occasionally Alfie was engaged for longer excursions into the Tavistock countryside, and at such times the remuneration he received was paltry in comparison to the physical demands made on him when negotiating steep hills. However there is no doubt he would have endured the physical hardship had he not also been subjected to severe bouts of religion where the invalid would extol the love and wonder of Jesus Christ.

On one particular day, when Alfie had pushed his client all the way up to 'The Pimple' (a local beauty 'spot') a raised feature on Whitchurch Down, he found that the incessant evangelical flow was too much for him to bear any longer. In a spontaneous outburst of protest, Alfie told the man, having first safely secured the brake of the wheelchair, that if Jesus were so b***** marvellous perhaps He would like to push him home to Tavistock for tuppence! Whereupon Alfie duly left the man high on the hill and walked back to Tavistock. Sometime, much later that day, the invalid was discovered and was safely returned to his home, none the worse for his ordeal, but perhaps just a little wiser in terms of human relationships.

Dartmoor Deaths

There are at least two 'famous' graves of suicide victims on Dartmoor: Jay who was 'with child' and in shame hung herself in a barn; and George Stephens who was forbidden to see his loved one so gorged himself to death on the poisonous leaves of Bella Donna or Deadly Nightshade. Both unfortunate characters, according to the law and practice at that time, had to be buried at the nearest crossroads (sign of the cross) as 'suicides' could not be buried in consecrated ground.

The method of internment was a spooky affair in itself. The grave had to be dug after dark and the coffin had to be buried by candlelight, without prayer or preaching. Jay is famous for having fresh flowers placed daily on her grave but poor George Stephens lies in a remote moorland location and gets few visitors.

House in a Day

Tom and Sally Satterley were newly weds at the end of George III's reign. Tom was an ostler at Two Bridges so, for people with such limited means, the likelihood of them ever owning their own property, however humble, was very remote. However Tom and Sally were aware that an ancient unwritten law existed to the effect that anyone who could construct a house in a single day, on common land, with smoke coming from the chimney, before the sun went down, would be entitled to keep it forever.

Naturally local landowners and dignitaries took a dim view of such proceedings; it encouraged the poorly paid working man to aspire to more than the scant existence to which he had grown accustomed! Tom and Sally therefore planned the whole operation with military precision.

The perfect opportunity arose on Midsummer's Day, about 1832, as the local gentry had an important date in their diaries – the celebrated Holne Ram Roasting ceremony, a social occasion which drew dignitaries from all over the moor.

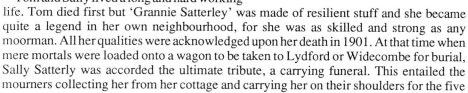

Tom and Sally had been stowing away building materials for several weeks and lived in fear of someone discovering them. Fortunately, none of their friends gave away the cunning plot and, as soon as the coast (and the moor!) was clear, they proceeded to build their single-storey cottage. All day they and their friends laboured, moving great granite stones to create a building which still stands to this day, believed to be the last 'house in a day' built cottage left in England.

Tom and Sally lived a long and hard working life. Tom died first but 'Grannie Satterley' was made of resilient stuff and she became quite a legend in her own neighbourhood, for she was as skilled and strong as any moorman. All her qualities were acknowledged upon her death in 1901. At that time when mere mortals were loaded onto a wagon to be taken to Lydford or Widecombe for burial, Sally Satterly was accorded the ultimate tribute, a carrying funeral. This entailed the mourners collecting her from her cottage and carrying her on their shoulders for the five

miles funeral procession to Widecombe.

Half way up Dartmeet Hill is a coffin stone. There was a tradition that a mason would carve the initials of the deceased onto the coffin stone or chisel a small cross. Sally's initials cannot be deciphered but, particularly in such an exposed location, the elements of wind and rain can easily weather any inscriptions. The men carrying Sally's coffin wore their Sunday best, complete with bowler hats. With many such funerals it was also a common occurrence for a bugler to greet the procession on Hameldon Hill, high above Widecombe, as another mark of respect.

Today Jolly Lane Cott remains on the right hand side of the steep hill which rises from Huccaby Bridge towards the Forest Inn on the road to Holne. Another storey was added at the beginning of the twentieth century and its relative fame has assured it of much attention.

A Fishy Tale

Bert Denham was a keen angler who was easily recognisable as, instead of sporting the normal fishing headgear, he would don a train driver's hat. One dark night he went fishing on a Dartmoor river, a short way downstream from the owner, a local squire. Although Bert had equipped himself with all the necessary paraphernalia for night fishing, the local landlord had forgotten his lamp. When he hooked a 'whopper', he called to Bert for assistance. It was only when some light was shed on the subject that it was discovered the prize catch was no giant trout or salmon – but a pink piglet which had been hooked by one of its ears. Fortunately it was landed safely, taken home and eventually recovered. It was unusual enough for a piglet to fall into a river – the chances of it being caught in this fashion, at night, must have been a million to one!

Rubbish!

Dartmoor is a beautiful place and nobody wants to see it submerged in litter like some of our city streets, but who would expect anyone to go to the lengths that a past owner of Prince Hall near Two Bridges went to? In 1936 Captain Llewellyn spotted a family dumping large amounts of litter on the moor. As they drove off he noted the car's registration. After some detective work, he managed to find out their home address in Yorkshire. He filled a tea chest with all the litter they had dropped – and sent it back to them with an appropriate note on how to conduct themselves in beautiful surroundings such as Dartmoor!

No Flies on This Fisherman!

An aristocratic gentleman went fishing at a Dartmoor reservoir. Unfortunately, whilst reeling in a fish, he stumbled and fell into deep water. Apart from his hat, he was soaked to the skin. Although most people in the same situation might call it a day, this gentleman was unfazed. He laid his clothes out to dry in the morning sunshine, and continued to fish, dressed only in his hat! There were few people around but, naturally, he was spotted; a pair of elderly nature enthusiasts were so shocked at this spectacle they reported him to the bailiff. A 'cover up' was ordered and he re-clothed himself sufficiently to avoid further embarrassment until dry clothes could be sent up from his hotel.

John Lee – the Man They Couldn't Hang

The 'legendary' John (Babbacombe) Lee manages to turn up in several of our books, mainly because his life story unfolded in so many localities (it starts near Newton Abbot, develops in Torquay, unfolds in Exeter and ends at Tavistock) and it is such a fascinating tale.

Briefly, in November 1884 at Babbacombe, now a part of Torquay, John Lee was accused of the murder of his employer, Emma Keyse, a rich and influential lady. The trial at Exeter was little more than a formality. This twenty-year-old from Abbotskerswell near Newton Abbot already had a prison record, and the sentencing judge was in no doubt as to his guilt.

In early 1885 John Lee was taken to the scaffold at Exeter. The hangman was the experienced James Berry, a man who was efficient at his grim trade. Three times Lee was placed on the scaffold, and three times the trap door mechanism failed to open, even though it was tested and worked in between times. The most peculiar aspect was that Lee had told the two warders looking after him that he had a dream that he wouldn't die, and this was noted in the logbook a day before the execution. He claimed that he wouldn't hang because he was innocent! His sentence was commuted to 'life' and he spent the next twenty two years in jail.

He was released from Portland, married Jessie Bulleid and had two daughters. He ended his days as a pauper in a Tavistock workhouse and is buried in a Tavistock cemetery, a place from which there is no escape – even for him.

Sugar and Spice?

Many years ago, about a mile downstream from Bellever and close to the banks of the East Dart River, there lived a pair of ladies at a house called White Slade. The scattered community of moor folk who lived in the district become curious as to how these ladies managed to live in such a remote spot with no visible means of supporting themselves, having no gardens and no animals. What is more they did not appear to patronise any of the surrounding farms which may have provided food. Despite this they were well covered, fat and buxom individuals and certainly well nourished. Things being what they were, the obvious conclusion was reached – they were witches. Rumours spread and many folk were keen to know the truth. Their cottage was watched most carefully and, when the ladies went out for some exercise, the locals seized the opportunity to go in to see what magic was brewing.

Everywhere they looked were jars of nature's products – berries, moorland fruit, slugs and snails. Although the ladies had done nothing wrong, they were greatly upset at being discovered. Within a few years they both died and White Slade, which had been nicknamed 'Snaily House', became a ruin.

What's in a Name?

In Lustleigh, a man whose surname was Flood had the nerve and strength of character to call his son Noah. The villagers automatically responded to this and renamed his house The Ark, a name which stayed with it for many years.

Cure for Whooping Cough – Dartmoor Medicine

Those with an interest in natural or homeopathic treatments for ills will find this remedy for whooping cough quite inventive. In 1852 a young child from Lustleigh, who was afflicted by this common complaint, was taken out, early one morning, to the fields. Here he was cuddled and cared for until a sheep awoke from her slumbers and got up. Immediately the child was taken and laid down on the same spot. He was told to lie face downwards and to inhale with his nostrils and his mouth as wide as was possible. This was done for some five minutes or so before he was gathered up and returned to his sick bed. We don't know whether the cure was forthcoming, but we do know the child made it through to manhood!

Another remedy against whooping cough is the regular eating of snails. Unfortunately this does increase the chances of contracting pulmonary tuberculosis. However the general public tends to be squeamish and the word 'ugh' seems to sum up the reaction to such foodstuffs.

Dartmoor's Exotic Wildlife

Most people's first impression of wildlife on Dartmoor would be the sweet little Dartmoor ponies featured so prominently on postcards and souvenirs. But Dartmoor is home to some far more exotic creatures, ranging from the harmless and timid wallaby, to the prickly porcupine.

The wallabies have been seen by people in the Teign Valley and near Haytor and are thought to have escaped from a private house many years ago. They have since adapted quite happily to life in our climate in much the same way as rabbits, grey squirrels, rats and house mice have done. The porcupines are more likely to have descended from a pair which disappeared from the Pine Valley Wildlife Park near Okehampton in the early 1970s. The species comes from the Himalayas and is strictly nocturnal but they do pose a problem for farmers as they cause damage to the trees by stripping bark, and they also threaten other species, particularly badgers.

If you had been around in the mid-nineteenth century you might have heard locals in villages like Lustleigh, on Eastern Dartmoor, referring to 'crocodiles'. Happily you are not likely to stumble over one of these creatures as they were actually referring to lizards! Not so happily for the lizards, though – they were considered worthy only of slaughter.

The Monster of Manaton

In the seventeenth century several people in the parish of Manaton were convinced of a monster lurking around the neighbourhood. It was snake-like in its appearance but had other appendages including legs, was bigger than an adult human being and had wings. It was particularly noisy as it went around the district terrorising the local populace and it is said that its hissing could be heard over a great distance.

Pecking the Parson

One winter at Lydford was particularly bad, the blizzard conditions of several days continuing to block lanes and make movement virtually impossible. Naturally the local schoolchildren had a whale of a time availing themselves of the snowy situation. However some of them were up to making mischief and one of the targets for their attentions was a goose heavily laden with eggs. Numerous times they disturbed her until the owner, Betty, decided enough was enough (or, as the French would say bearing in mind the state of the goose, 'an œuf is an œuf').

The quietest place she could find was the village church; the parson had been unable to hold services on

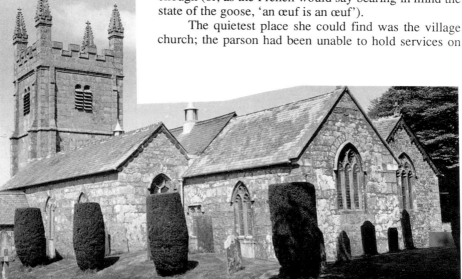

three consecutive Sundays and there was little sign of the weather relenting. And the ideal spot was the pulpit. Here she prepared a cosy nest and, duly comfortably settled in, the goose laid thirteen eggs.

But then the weather took a turn for the better and a sequence of warmer days melted away the snow. Betty, aware that the parson could now hold a service, was panic-stricken. The parson, on hearing the story, decided to go ahead with the service as the parishioners could be seen wending their way to church. He told Betty that he would simply straddle the goose as there was easily room for one foot either side of her. All went well whilst the parson gave out various notices, but as soon as he tried to preach from the pulpit the goose started to hiss loudly. The rest, as they say, is all 'hissstory' as the parson was pecked so persistently on his unprotected calves he had to abandon the service. The victorious goose produced the goslings, and normality then returned to the church.

Low Calorie Golf Balls

A bullock grazing at Okehampton's golf course showed distinct signs of deterioration of health, which baffled both the farmer and the vet. Despite intensive treatment the poor creature became so poorly that he had to be put down. An autopsy revealed that he had died as a result of chronic 'golf ballitus' having consumed no less than forty six of them!

At Tavistock it was the human members of the golf club who were suffering. They could not understand why their practice area for putting, an immaculate strip, was showing obvious signs of damage. Between their practice area and the open moorland and commons of Whitchurch Down, there was a short fence, a closed gate and a cattle grid. However a night watch revealed that a clever moorland pony had learnt how to undo the

latch on the gate and let himself in to dine. The remedy was simple, a padlock on the gate and the problem was solved.

But it wasn't, because the bordering plants and flowers and the practice area continued to be damaged. Another night watch followed and the dismayed onlooker saw the offending pony approach the cattle grid, lie down, roll over then right itself again on the club house side!

The Man Who Wasn't Outfoxed

H.G. Hurrell, whose father was Mayor of Plymouth on no less than three occasions, was an acknowledged expert in wildlife, a man with great vision and energy involved with many organisations. Many audiences appreciated his work and the energy and enthusiasm he put into it.

Anyone who has ever risked life and limb to capture a 'perfect picture' with their camera will sympathise with and appreciate what he went through in order to obtain a desired photographic film sequence.

He had set his heart on filming a fox attacking a sheep. Despite his constant forays into the countryside on the southern edge of Dartmoor, he could not capture the appropriate scene on film. But H.G. refused to give in and he devised a 'cunning plan'. He obtained the fleece of a sheep and disguised himself as one of the flock. It is not known how long he spent in this pursuit before finally succeeding, but it is known that in the quest he was almost rounded up by a sheepdog!

Tavistock Goosie Fair

Tavistock Goosie Fair is an important date in the Dartmoor calendar although the days have long since gone when there were thousands of geese marched, on foot, into town. There would be great competition for the best pens, for that meant the geese were in front when the bidding was at its most enthusiastic. Dinah Tuckett, a well known moorman from Dunnabridge Pound near Two Bridges, would leave her farm at midnight to be in Tavistock at 4 a.m. simply in order to secure the best pens.

It was a buoyant market, a scene of colour and noise. It was a time for buying, selling and settling debts. It was also a time for renewing old friendships. Even farmers who had no business to conduct would make every effort to get along – although they might have had to resort to some matrimonial deception. One ploy was to select an animal, a ram or a horse that the farmer did not particularly wish to sell, and head off towards Tavistock. Along the way he would visit a pub, have a drink, and deposit his animal in an adjacent field. He would then attend the Goosie Fare, avail himself of the all day opening of pubs and the socialising, then collect the animal on the return journey it 'not having made the required price'.

But not all the folk who visited the fair had an association with the agricultural aspects of the show, for the fun fairs, stalls and other attractions drew people from all over the South West, and from all walks of life. Until the demise of the railway to Tavistock, the town would be flooded with sailors from Devonport and Plymouth. Many were intent on a good time and, inevitably, ended up much the worse for drink. In anticipation of this, many of the town's landlords would unscrew and remove any doors in the pub so they could throw out the worst offenders more easily. No small wonder that the biggest and burliest policeman in Devon were also drafted in. The sailors' problems didn't end there, though. Tavistock had two railway stations and it was quite common for sailors to be despatched in the wrong direction so, instead of returning to their ship in good time, they would be marooned in Exeter.

Annie Pinkham's Men

If you travel the A386 road from Okehampton to Tavistock you will pass the industrial remains of the Wheal Betsy Mine, a most distinct landmark left as a visible reminder of the days when Dartmoor had a substantial number of mines. Along the roadside edge are a great number of stones which prevent people pulling onto the side. These have become known as 'Annie Pinkham's Men'.

It appears that Annie lived at Peter Tavy, a village about a mile to the south of Wheal Betsy, but went in to service at a large house in the Lydford area, a few miles to the north of Wheal Betsy. When she had time off she would return home on foot, passing 'her men' en route. She would tell locals that she had seen them and would often joke that they had waved or spoken to her as she passed by.

Amen

In the parish of Manaton, but a few miles from its church, is the Heathercombe Estate located on the leeward side of the great ridge of Hameldown. For a long while it was a Christian School. In the late 1960s and early 1970s three stones were erected by the estate's owner to echo his concern about the abuse of power throughout the world. As fishes appear on these stones, they are often referred to as the Fishes Stones, each being about five feet high. One is engraved 'Thine is the Kingdom', another 'Thine is the Power' and, as you have probably already guessed, the last of the trilogy says 'Thine is the Glory'.

'Amen' to that!